WORLD IN PERIL

FORESTS
UNDER THREAT

PAUL MASON

Heinemann Library

www.heinemannraintree.com

Visit our website to find out more information about Heinemann-Raintree books.

To order:

☎ Phone 888-454-2279

💻 Visit www.heinemannraintree.com to browse our catalog and order online.

© 2009 Heinemann Library
an imprint of Capstone Global Library, LLC
Chicago, Illinois

Customer Service: 888-454-2279

Visit our website at www.heinemannraintree.com

Edited by Louise Galpine and Rachel Howells
Designed by Richard Parker and Manhattan Design
Picture research by Hannah Taylor and Rebecca Sodergren
Production by Alison Parsons

Printed in China by Leo Paper Products Ltd.

13 12 11 10 09
10 9 8 7 6 5 4 3 2 1

Library of Congress Cataloging-in-Publication Data
Mason, Paul.
  Forests under threat / Paul Mason. -- 1st ed.
    p. cm. -- (World in peril)
  Includes bibliographical references and index.
  ISBN 978-1-4329-2288-7 (hc) -- ISBN 978-1-4329-2295-5 (pb)
  1. Deforestation--Juvenile literature. 2. Forest conservation--Juvenile literature. 3. Nature--Effect of human beings on--Juvenile literature. I. Title.

  SD418.M37 2009
  333.75--dc22

                        2008037072

Acknowledgments

We would like to thank the following for permission to reproduce photographs: Alamy pp. **8** (Lee Foster), **13** (Terry Whittaker), **27** (Steve Atkins Photography); Corbis pp. **7** (Martin Harvey), **9** (epa/ Martin Alipaz), **15** (John and Lisa Merrill); Corbis Sygma p. **23** (Yves Forestier); FLPA pp. **18** (Imagebroker/ ROM), **19** (Frans Lanting); FLPA/ Minden Pictures/ Mark Moffett p. **17** (FLPA); Getty Images p. **16** (Will and Deni McIntyre); Paul Mason p. **25**; Photolibrary pp. **6** (Nordic Photos), **11** (Corbis), **14** (Douglas Peebles), **20** (Lynn Stone), **24** (David Clapp); Reuters pp. **12** (Gregg Newton), **26** (Christophe Karaba); Science Photo Library p. **21** (Will and Deni McIntyre); SIME-4Corners Images p. **4** (Johannah Huber); Still Pictures pp. **10** (Hartmut Schwarzbach), **22** (Jeff Henry).

Cover photograph of cutting in tropical rain forest, Panama, reproduced with permission of Corbis (Frans Lanting).

We would like to thank Michael Mastrandrea for his invaluable help in the preparation of this book.

Every effort has been made to contact copyright holders of material reproduced in this book. Any omissions will be rectified in subsequent printings if notice is given to the publishers.

All the Internet addresses (URLs) given in this book were valid at the time of going to press. However, due to the dynamic nature of the Internet, some addresses may have changed, or sites may have changed or ceased to exist since publication. While the author and publishers regret any inconvenience this may cause readers, no responsibility for any such changes can be accepted by either the author or the publishers.

Contents

Some words are printed in bold, **like this**. You can find out what they mean by looking in the glossary.

What Makes Forests So Important?

At one time, forests covered two-thirds of the land on Earth. Millions of different insects, plants, and animals lived among the trees. This great variety of living things is called **biodiversity**.

There are many different types of forest. In cold regions, huge forests of evergreen trees stretch so far that it takes days to travel through them. Farther south, the trees grow more thinly and **shed** their leaves in winter. Near the **equator**, the forests can be so thick that travelers have to cut plants down to clear their path.

Throughout history, forest plants and animals have been a source of food for people. Wood for building and heating has come from forests. Many medicines first came from forest plants.

Our planet's population is growing fast, and our demands on the forests are also increasing. Today, only 30 percent of land is covered in forest. Half our forests have already been cut down—and the remaining forests are under threat.

How Does This Forest Help the Planet Survive?

Imagine what it would be like to drift through the rain forest along this river. Like all forests, the rain forest is a crucial part of life on Earth. The trees take in the gas carbon dioxide, which helps them grow. They release oxygen, which humans and other animals need to survive. Because they breathe in carbon dioxide and breathe out oxygen, forests are sometimes called "the lungs of the planet."

Rain forest trees such as this take years to grow, but just a few minutes to cut down. In the last 70 years, more than half the world's tropical rain forests have been cut down. There are now fewer trees to absorb carbon dioxide than there have been for thousands of years.

Without trees, less carbon dioxide is removed from the air. The extra carbon dioxide stops heat from escaping from Earth. As a result, Earth's average temperature rises. This is called **global warming**.

What Happens When Trees Are Cut Down?

How long would it take you to get soaked in this kind of rain? It is called the rain forest for a reason—it rains a lot! The Amazon basin is home to about 20 percent of the world's fresh water. The trees suck water from the soil up through their roots. They release **water vapor** into the air through their leaves. The water is **recycled** into Earth's atmosphere, forming clouds. The clouds later release the water as rain.

These floods are in the Beni region of the Bolivian rain forest. What caused the floods? If trees are cut down in rain forest areas, there are fewer tree roots to suck the water out of the soil. Instead the soil becomes **waterlogged**, which causes floods. The water is not recycled into the air. As the water washes down through the soil instead, it pushes the **nutrients** deeper and deeper down. Eventually, it becomes impossible for more trees or other plants to grow on the cleared land.

This woman in Laos is growing crops in a small forest garden. Her ancestors have lived in forests for hundreds of years. They have always planted such gardens, without causing any long-term damage. Several different crops are planted together. Each plant takes a different kind of **nutrient** from the soil, leaving some behind. In this way, some nutrients remain.

This giant farm has been carved out of the rain forest. Every year, huge areas of forest in South America, Africa, and Asia are cleared for farmland. Often they are used to grow corn or for cattle farming. Corn crops quickly use up the soil's nutrients. Once the nutrients are gone, the crops can only be grown on the land if farmers use chemical **fertilizers** on the soil. These are expensive and can harm the **environment**.

How Does Slash-and-Burn Affect the Rain Forest?

In most forest areas, the soil does not contain many **nutrients**. If the same crop is grown on it year after year, the soil's nutrients are quickly used up. Because of this, rain forest people such as the Yanomami Indians (pictured) use **slash-and-burn** farming. They cut down the trees and burn the plants to clear land. After a few years of growing crops, they move to a new place. In time, the trees and plants come back and the soil recovers.

This is a much larger area of land than the Yanomami would clear. Many poor people come to the rain forest hoping to make a better life. They clear large areas like this for slash-and-burn farming. But instead of moving on after a few years, they settle down. Each year the soil loses more nutrients and produces less food. In the end, nothing can grow on the land—not even the trees that once stood there.

Trees are not only cut down to make room for farms. They are also cut down to sell the wood. This is a *koa* tree on the Hawaiian island of Kauai. Its wood is very valuable.

Koa is a **hardwood**, like mahogany, birch, walnut, and maple. Makers of furniture and musical instruments often use hardwoods in their work. *Koa* is especially popular with makers of ukuleles.

Who would have guessed that the tree on the left might become an instrument like the one above? Hardwood instruments such as this ukulele are said to have a better sound than other, cheaper woods.

In poor areas of Asia and South America, hardwood forests are now being cut down in large numbers. This is because hardwoods are so valuable. Today, some types of tree are in danger of disappearing altogether.

How Does Logging Affect Forest Animals?

Forests are very complicated places. The plants and animals that live in them are all connected to one another. For example, in the rain forest, birds called toucans eat mostly fruit. They then release the fruit seeds in their droppings. Without enough toucans to spread the seeds around, the rain forests would suffer a shortage of fruit trees. Toucans and other animals that eat fruit would go hungry.

How much space is left for the animals that live in this patch of forest? When large areas of forest are cut down, animals have less space to roam in. Finding homes, food, and mates becomes harder. The weaker animals will die out and numbers will shrink.

Rare plants and flowers are also affected. With fewer plants around, insects are less likely to visit them. The plants are not **pollinated**, so they do not **reproduce**. The richness of forest life is lessened.

Why Can't This Orangutan Find Love?

Why might this male orangutan in Borneo be looking a little grumpy? Orangutans once lived in forests throughout Southeast Asia and China. Male orangutans roamed large areas, looking for a female to mate with. Because they had giant forests to search through, finding a female was easy. Today, finding a mate is much harder.

This photograph shows **logging** in Sabah, Borneo. As forests like this one are cut down, orangutans have less and less space to live in. This is called **habitat loss**. With only a small area to live in, it is hard for orangutans to find homes, food, and mates.

Today, orangutans are an **endangered species**. There are so few of them that there is a risk they will die out completely.

How Does Acid Rain Kill Habitats?

This Siberian tiger is lying in the thick, evergreen forests known as **boreal forests**. Boreal forests spread in a circle across North America, northern Europe, and Asia.

Sometimes the **canopy** is so thick that it is dark under the trees, even in daylight. Even so, the forests are home to wolves, bald eagles, bears, Siberian tigers, and many rare plants.

Would you like to get caught in rain that can strip leaves off trees? The Siberian tiger and its fellow creatures do not have a choice. Many boreal forests are affected by acid rain, which is caused by **pollution** getting into the air. The pollution mixes with the **water vapor** in clouds to form acid. When water vapor falls as rain, the acid comes down, too. It kills trees and other plants and also harms the soil. Sometimes the acid even gets into drinking water. The **habitats** of many rare animals who live in boreal forests are at risk.

What Causes Forest Fires?

This forest in Yellowstone National Park, in the northwestern United States, is recovering from the effects of a fire. Many forest areas need fires. The flames clear away the forest **canopy**, allowing light to flood the forest floor and helping new plants to grow there.

Some trees are triggered into releasing their seeds by fire. Forest plants may have **fire-resistant** seeds, reserve roots that sprout after a fire, or bark that is not affected by fires.

This fire in southern France happened when someone threw away
a lit cigarette. Today, some forests are suffering from too many fires.
It takes time for plants to grow and animals to return after a fire.
If there is another fire too soon, the forest cannot cope.

Campers lighting barbecue grills and people throwing away lit
cigarettes cause hundreds of fires each year. Some fires are even
started deliberately by people to clear the land for farming.

What Happens When Logged Trees Are Replaced?

Natural woodland, like this bluebell wood in Hampshire, England, takes years to develop. It is home to all sorts of different plants and animals.

What happens when woods like this one are cut down? New trees are sometimes planted. Usually they are evergreen trees. Evergreens grow faster than the old trees they have replaced. This means that they can be cut down for timber much sooner.

Imagine how scary it would be to find your way through a dark forest like this one at night! It is not only humans who find forests like this unwelcoming. Compared to the old forest, there are fewer plants and bushes for insects, small animals, and birds to live among. The **habitat** has changed, and the original animals are not **adapted** to life here. Many either leave for new areas or die out.

How Can We Help Forests Survive?

These protesters are trying to stop **logging** in Asia. The tiger and orangutan suits represent two of the many animals that suffer when forests are destroyed. But can our forests be saved?

Small areas of forest are now officially protected. This stops logging and prevents land from being cleared to make farms. Around the world, fewer than 15 percent of forests are protected. If all unprotected forests were cut down, it would be disastrous.

What can you do to help save the forests? Each year, forests are cut down to make paper. Using less paper, and **recycling** the paper you do use, is a good way to help save our forests. Reusing old wood, like these doors, also helps. Make sure any new wood you use comes from a **sustainable** source. Most sustainable wood is advertised as such, because then more people are aware that by buying it, they can help save forests.

WHAT DID YOU FIND OUT ABOUT FORESTS?

How do the world's forests keep us all alive?
Hint: The phrase "lungs of the planet" should help you. Also, try going back to pages 6–7 for an explanation.

How many different types of forest can you see in this book? Where in the world are they?
Hint: Among them might be rain forests, evergreen **boreal forests**, forests where the trees **shed** their leaves in winter, and mountain forests. Pages 6, 7, 8, 9, 10, 11, 12, 13, and 20 give a few examples.

Make a list of the different things humans get from forests.
Hint: Some of them might be immediately obvious, such as wood. Others might be less obvious—what about fresh air and paper, for example?

What are the different threats facing our forests today?
Hint: You do not only have to include direct threats like **logging**. If trees are cut down to make room for cattle farms, maybe the threat is really our demand for meat?

When trees are cut down, do floods become more or less likely? Why is this? Can anything else grow on the flooded soil afterward?
Hint: Look at the photograph on page 9 that shows just a few trees, but a lot of water.

What does cutting down trees do to the soil?
Hint: Look at the photographs on pages 9–11 and 13 to find some answers. It is what happens beneath the surface of the soil that is important.

What are the costs of saving our forests?

Hint: Try to think of the ways our lives would have to change if we stopped cutting down trees tomorrow. Are there ways in which life would get harder for ordinary people around the world?

What are the benefits of saving our forests?

Hint: There are both obvious and hidden answers to this question. See the chapters throughout the book for answers, but page 5 should provide a helpful summary.

Can you think of any disadvantages to helping to save the forests? Is it possible that there could ever be too many trees on the planet?

Hint: Could leaving our trees alone actually damage the environment? Do you think you would be able to notice the difference?

What are some things you can do to help save the forests?

Hint: Some of them might not be obvious. For example, could what you eat have an effect on the forests? Or perhaps the kind of transportation you use? Or even whether you leave the lights on in an empty room? Page 27 might give you some ideas.

adapt how a plant or animal changes over time to survive in its habitat

biodiversity range of different living things in an environment. An area's biodiversity includes its animals, plants, fungi, and bacteria.

boreal forest forest in an area with cold, often snowy winters and warm summers. The trees in boreal forests are often evergreens, which keep their leaves all year round.

canopy cover created when the tops of trees grow together, blocking out light

endangered species any type of living thing that is in danger of dying out

environment landscape, soil, weather, plants, and animals that together make one place different from another

equator imaginary line that runs around the center of Earth. The weather is usually hot and wet around the equator.

fertilizer chemical added to soil to help plants grow. Chemicals washed off the soil and into rivers can affect the plants and animals that live there.

fire-resistant able to survive even if there is a fire

global warming rise in Earth's average temperature

habitat local environment, which is home to particular types of plants and animals

habitat loss destruction of a particular type of habitat. The livi things that normally live there ha either less space or no space left.

hardwood wood from trees that their leaves each year before win

logging cutting down of trees fo wood, usually to make money

nutrient combination of chemica that is needed for living things to grow or repair themselves. Plants some of their nutrients from the s they grow in.

pollinate help to reproduce, by v from insects

pollution dirt that harms the environment

recycled when something is use again to make a new product

reproduce make offspring or you When dogs have puppies, they ar reproducing.

shed get rid of. Some trees shed leaves each year before winter.

slash-and-burn farming that invo cutting and burning forests to clea land, then planting crops. Traditio the land is only used to grow crop a few years. The farmers then mo to a new piece of land.

sustainable produced in a way th does not harm the environment

waterlogged full of water

water vapor gas form of water

Find Out More

Books

Ganeri, Anita. *World Cultures: Living in the Amazon Rain Forest*. Chicago: Raintree, 2008.

Pyers, Greg. *Habitat Explorer: Rain Forest Explorer*. Chicago: Raintree, 2005.

Sharman, Helen. *Eye Wonder: Rainforest*. New York: Dorling Kindersley, 2001.

Telford, Carole, and Rod Theodorou. *Amazing Journeys: Up a Rainforest Tree*. Chicago: Heinemann Library, 2006.

Websites

www.panda.org/news_facts/education/middle_school/habitats/temperate_forests

and

www.panda.org/news_facts/education/middle_school/habitats/coniferous_forests

and

www.panda.org/news_facts/education/middle_school/habitats/tropical_forests

Together, these are the WWF's web pages on temperate, coniferous, and tropical forests. Each page is full of information about forests and also offers links to related subjects.

www.greenpeace.org/usa/campaigns/forests

This section of the **environmental** group Greenpeace's website is about forests. You can follow links to explore forests in North America, forests worldwide, and more. This web page also includes a useful section listing recent news developments about forests.

Index